The RAF Battle of Britain Memorial Flight (BBMF) Spitfire Mk VB on its final approach to the grass runway at Audley End in Essex, England. Audley End is the home of Historic Flying Ltd., a premier Spitfire restoration facility.

Ron Dick

AVM, RAF

Designed by Dan Patterson. Edited by Ross A. Howell, Jr. and Jamie L. Bronner.

Library of Congress Catalog
Card Number 97-75156

ISBN 1-57427-071-0

Printed in Hong Kong

Published by Howell Press, Inc., 1147 River Road, Suite 2, Charlottesville, VA 22901 Telephone 804-977-4006

First Printing

HOWELL PRESS

Previous page: At the left center of the photograph, a pilot's knee clipboard rests under an escape map printed on silk and a flare pistol with cartridge. At top left is the woolen battle dress jacket of an enlisted pilot with Canada patch, a symbol of the combined war effort of the Commonwealth. A pilot's flight helmet, goggles, and oxygen mask rest atop the fleece-lined Irvin jacket necessary for high-altitude operations. An officer's cap and flight boots are at the right. In the center are Spitfire Pilot Notes *under a black cigarette case. Resting atop the case are embroidered pilot's wings. The small blue patch with the winged goldfish and two waves denotes the survivor of two bailouts and rescue from the waters between England and the continent.*

The silhouette of a Spitfire Mk IX in the foreground with the BBMF's Mk VB behind it in the sun.

The fin of the BBMF Spitfire Mk IIA, RAF Coningsby.

Preface

When I was in the UK to make the photographs for this book, I had the chance to shoot air-to-air photos of the Spitfire Mk IX and the Messerschmitt Bf 109 on the same flight. As this possibility evolved into a real opportunity and the logistics and schedules began to fall into place, I once again started to feel how lucky I have been to be in the right place at the right time and to have met the right people. Every time I get to climb into a World War II airplane and go flying, I remind myself that what I see and what I photograph is for the reader, the viewer of these books.

On September 14, 1996, after the flight from the previous day had been canceled due to unfavorable winds, the photo flight was about to happen. The Spitfire and Bf 109 were in France, performing a dual display at an air show over the Channel Islands. We were to meet them over the English Channel as they returned from a fuel stop just across the Channel from Folkestone. The pilot, Martin Sergeant, and I were to circle in his T-6 at 3,500 feet, just out over the water from the white cliffs that are so recognizable as England.

The call came from France; Clive Denney, flying the Spitfire—they were on their way. We took off. The September afternoon was just about perfect. The sky was clear and the visibility unrestricted. The sun had that low-angle, golden quality that makes a photographer's job easy. As we flew towards the coast, the castles and villages of Kent unrolled beneath the wings, the large chalk figure of a horse drawn into a hillside was clearly visible off the left wing...an icon from a far earlier age. We circled at the agreed-upon altitude, the French coast just visible to the east.

We circled over the Battle of Britain Memorial that sits atop the cliffs, an earthwork that forms a three-bladed propeller. On the radio Martin tells me that they are incoming...there they are...flying a loose formation just below the clouds...a Spitfire and a Messerschmitt. It is the weekend that the UK celebrates the Battle of Britain. As the two fighters approach, they form up into a tight two-ship flight. The Spitfire leading, they dive for the Memorial. As they cross over the top of the cliffs, the shadows of the fighters race across the ground..."wow, they are really low." Then I lost sight of them, reminding me how difficult aerial combat must be. We continued to circle to let them find us.

What happened next, I will never forget. I was looking from side to side, trying to find the fighters, when they suddenly appeared, like apparitions from another time. One on each side of the T-6, the Spitfire and the Messerschmitt. With the roar of the big radial engine up front, the two fighters had seemingly silently appeared, climbing into formation with the T-6 and matching our speed, just hanging there. Before I began my work, I took just a moment to appreciate what I was a part of and how lucky I am. Two fighters that were opponents, now together, in the airspace where one of the most famous air battles in history took place, on the weekend that the victorious country celebrates that battle, and one lucky guy from Ohio.

I went to work.

Dan Patterson
August 18, 1997

SPITFIRE

RAF Fighter

Photographs by Dan Patterson

Text by Air Vice-Marshal Ron Dick

Howell Press

The Supermarine S.6B.

NASM

Whenever the great aircraft of aviation's first century are discussed, the name Spitfire is certain to be among those mentioned. Supermarine's splendid fighter would be remembered for the classical elegance of its lines, if for nothing else. With its slim fuselage set on gracefully curved elliptical wings, the Spitfire was a raving beauty from the start. There was more to it than that, however—much more. The attractive appearance of its airframe was matched by the Spitfire's remarkable performance and great potential for development. Upon its introduction to service, the Spitfire became the Royal Air Force's foremost fighter, and it retained its dominance in the RAF's front line throughout the era of the piston-engined monoplane. More than 20,000 of all variants were built, and from its earliest days it came to be thought of as the fighter pilot's ideal, an irresistible combination of power, grace, and combat effectiveness. Douglas Bader, the RAF's celebrated legless fighter leader, said of the Spitfire: "Here was the aeroplane *par excellence*...in fact, the aeroplane of one's dreams."

The Spitfire took on a wider significance, too. For the British people in the dark early days of World War II, the aircraft and its name acquired an almost mystic quality. Although not then the RAF's most numerous fighter, the Spitfire caught the public imagination like no other instrument of war and became a symbol of the nation's defiance, a standard-bearer pointing the way to eventual victory.

Lineage of a Legend

The Spitfire was born in the mind of a uniquely talented engineer. Reginald Mitchell was appointed Chief Designer of the Supermarine Aviation Works in 1919, when he was only twenty-four. During the 1920s, he was principally involved with the design of marine aircraft of one kind or another. A Supermarine biplane flying boat, the chubby little Sea Lion, won the Schneider Trophy race in 1922, and that led to greater things. In 1925, Mitchell's exceptionally clean floatplane, the S.4, set a world record for floatplanes of 226 MPH, but crashed into Chesapeake Bay after developing wing flutter at the outset of that year's Schneider Trophy competition. Undeterred, Mitchell went on to produce the S.5, S.6, and S.6B floatplanes which won the races held in 1927, 1929, and 1931, thereby gaining the Schneider Trophy outright for Britain. The S.6B also became the first aircraft to register speeds above 400 MPH when it set a World Air Speed record of 407 MPH. Given the considerable drag of huge floats and assorted bracing wires, that was a remarkable achievement. Mitchell learned a lot about the problems of high-speed flight from the Schneider Trophy experience, and that hard won knowledge was of great value in later years, although it would be an exaggeration to say that the fighters which followed were linked to his racing floatplanes by a continuous thread of design.

In 1928, Supermarine was absorbed by the larger Vickers company, but the merger had little immediate effect on Mitchell and his team. Then, in 1931, the Air Ministry in London issued Specification F7/30 for a fighter to replace the RAF's Bristol Bulldog, a delightful little biplane with a performance not significantly better than its World War I predecessors. Seven aircraft companies offered a varied selection of eight designs—five biplanes and three monoplanes. Supermarine's entry was the Type 224, a novel all-metal low-winged monoplane with the most powerful engine available, the 660 HP Rolls-Royce Goshawk. Here was a more obvious link with the development work done for the Schneider Trophy. The Rolls-Royce engineers had provided the racing engines for Mitchell's floatplanes and had learned many lessons which were carried forward in a series of designs, culminating in the famous Merlin, the power plant used in the Hurricane, Mosquito, Lancaster, and P-51 Mustang, as well as the Spitfire.

Unpleasant memories of flutter on the S.4 still lingered in Mitchell's mind, and the design for his venture into the fighter world was relatively conservative. The cranked wing of the Type 224 was uncompromisingly thick, its cockpit was open, and heavy spats shrouded its fixed undercarriage. The performance figures were correspondingly disappointing—238 MPH top speed and eight minutes to reach 15,000 ft. Troubles with the evaporatively cooled Goshawk compounded the Type 224's problems, and the RAF chose the safer option of the Gloster Gladiator, an agile radial-engined biplane which recorded a top speed of over 240 MPH and could reach 15,000 ft in six and a half minutes. Despite the disappointment, fighter development work continued at Supermarine. The Type 300 was based on the 224, but was a much cleaner shape. It had a closed cockpit, straightened wings, and retractable landing gear. It still proposed using the Goshawk, however, and its projected top speed

NASM

Reginald Mitchell and Henry Royce.

10

was only 265 MPH. Better things followed in November 1934, when it was suggested that further development of the airframe should be based on using a new Rolls-Royce engine, the PV XII. Although still suffering from teething troubles, the twenty-seven-liter PV XII (later named Merlin) showed great promise, its target output even at that early stage being 1,000 HP. Convinced by Mitchell's recommendations, the Vickers board approved the necessary money to proceed with detailed designs, and within a month the Air Ministry had issued a contract for the production of a prototype fighter. This was followed in January 1935 by Specification F37/34, largely written around Mitchell's proposal.

The Spitfire Takes Shape

In moving to the next stage, Mitchell had to take a number of things into consideration—most notably, that the Merlin engine was much heavier than the Goshawk, and that the thickness/chord ratio of the wing had to be kept as small as possible while accommodating the undercarriage and the guns. The various factors drove him inexorably towards an elliptical shape as the most practical solution, and the famous Spitfire planform finally appeared on paper. In due course, clever design work produced a wing which was very strong, but lighter and thinner than that of any other fighter of the time. It also embodied "washout," a twist in the wing which reduced its angle of incidence by 2½ degrees from root to tip. In tight turns, so much a feature of close combat, that meant that the root would stall before the tip, giving the pilot a warning buffet and allowing him to avoid any tendency for the aircraft to flick out of the turn. Riding on the edge of the buffet, the Spitfire could maintain the tightest possible turns, while keeping clear of the stall and maintaining full aileron control. This "honest" behavior was to prove of inestimable value to pilots in combat throughout the war.

As the Supermarine team developed its designs, the Air Ministry amplified its ideas in new specifications. Among other things, F10/35 stated that eight guns were desirable, each with 300 rounds of ammunition. These were incorporated by Mitchell, as was a cut in the fuel requirements which allowed the prototype to be fitted with tankage for only 75 gallons. Projected takeoff weight was thereby reduced and climb performance improved, enhancing the fighter's qualities as a short range interceptor at the expense of its

The Spitfire prototype.

reach. At the time, the problems of defending the skies over Britain loomed much larger than any possible future need for penetration of enemy airspace.

As work on the prototype gained momentum, Mitchell's basic design changed very little, but nevertheless improvements were made. The fuselage lengthened a little, the wingspan shrank a bit, the tail plane was raised a few inches, the wings were given increased dihedral, and the cockpit grew more glazing behind the pilot's head. The problem of dissipating the enormous quantity of heat produced by the Rolls-Royce engine was solved in two ways. Ethylene glycol, which has a much higher boiling point than water, was used as a coolant, and a ducted radiator was designed which not only cooled efficiently but also provided a small amount of additional thrust as it expelled its heated air.

By early 1936, the prototype was almost ready and the Air Ministry was impatient to see it fly. It was learned that the RAF was to receive 900 of the new monoplane fighters. Some 600 of these would be Hurricanes supplied by Hawker Aircraft, and it was planned that the remainder would come from Supermarine. The Vickers management said that they expected to complete contractor's trials by the end of March, and, provided service trials were over by the end of April and firm orders placed, production of the fighter, at a rate of five per week, could start by

September 1937. As is often the case, the company's confident forecasts were to prove unduly optimistic.

The Prototype Airborne

During the first week of March 1937, Supermarine's F37/34 prototype (Serial No. K5054), its engine runs satisfactory, was pronounced ready for flight testing. It had been taken from the factory at Woolston, near Southampton, to Eastleigh airfield to await its test pilot. There is some confusion over the date of the first flight, but it seems most probable that it was March 5. That morning, K5054 sat out on Eastleigh's grass under clear skies, unpainted save for RAF markings, and was photographed from every angle. Some time after lunch, the Chief Test Pilot of Vickers, "Mutt" Summers, climbed into the cockpit. Engine checks completed, he moved off to the far side of the airfield, turned into the wind, and took off. The fighter climbed away to a safe altitude for Summers to carry out some basic handling—checking the stalling speed and the effect of controls. For the first flight, the undercarriage was locked down, so no high speed flying was possible. Twenty minutes later, he landed, taxied in, and shut down. "I don't want anything touched," he said from the cockpit. It was a remark which many present took to mean that the aircraft was perfect as it stood, which was far from the case. Much serious testing and modifying lay

Spitfire Mark I.

ahead. Nevertheless, it was an indication that there was nothing drastically wrong with K5054, and that in itself was cause for celebration.

In the months that followed, the flight test program progressed satisfactorily, disturbed only occasionally by minor incidents. K5054 was given a coat of light blue paint, finished to immaculate smoothness by men who worked on Rolls-Royce cars. A level true speed of 349 MPH at 16,800 ft was recorded and the limiting indicated airspeed of 380 MPH was reached in a dive. A height of 34,700 ft was achieved. The prototype was flown by a number of test pilots, both company and RAF, none of whom had any difficulty in adapting to the new fighter and generally found that it handled pleasantly. On the strength of their reports, it was decided that the average RAF pilot should be able to cope with the aircraft and the Air Ministry confirmed an initial order for 310 of the type.

While his creation went from strength to strength, Mitchell waned visibly. He was suffering from an incurable cancer and it had reached an advanced stage. He did not allow his deteriorating health to deter him, however. He still visited the factory or went to see the aircraft whenever he could, and his spirit seemed undimmed. A typically forthright comment burst out of him when he heard that the Air Ministry had accepted the name Spitfire for the fighter: "Spitfire! It's the sort of bloody silly name they would give it." On June 11,1937, at the age of forty-two, Reginald Mitchell died, having seen to

it that his aircraft was well established on the road to success. It was a legacy for which his country would have cause to be forever grateful.

The latter period of K5054's flying life was not always untroubled. Several incidents brought anxious moments. One RAF test pilot on his first flight in the new fighter forgot to lower the undercarriage until the last minute and almost landed wheels up. Supermarine's test pilot, Jeffrey Quill, saw the oil pressure drop to zero just after taking off for a press day display and was hard-pressed to get the aircraft back on the airfield before the engine seized. The engine actually did fail on March 22, 1937, and the pilot had to put the aircraft down on its belly in open farmland, both man and machine remarkably free from serious hurt. The inadequacy of K5054's pneumatic system was revealed when a pilot conducting night flying trials ran out of air for the flaps and brakes after being forced to use an excessive amount of air in taxiing downwind. The ensuing touchdown was both long and fast, and the prototype ran off the end of the runway, finally nosing over in soft ground to end once more only slightly damaged. More seriously, on March 23, 1938, a heavy night landing led to the shearing of an undercarriage leg and substantial damage. It was July 19 before the necessary repairs, together with some modifications, were complete and the aircraft was available to continue test flying.

Once the first production Spitfires appeared starting in May 1938, K5054's role in the development program grew less vital, but the

prototype still had its uses and was flown regularly until September 1939. Then, on September 4, the day after Britain declared war on Nazi Germany, K5054 was involved in a fatal accident. Flight Lieutenant "Spinner" White landed the little fighter heavily at Farnborough; it bounced several times, then nosed over to fall on its back. White died later from his injuries and K5054 was never repaired.

Teething Troubles

The prototype had served its purpose in blazing a trail for more than 20,000 Spitfires to follow, and it had shown that the average pilot, using his head and sticking to the rules, should generally have little difficulty in coping with a high performance monoplane. As the RAF handling trials report said: "The aeroplane is simple and easy to fly and has no vices." Simple though the Spitfire might be to fly, producing it in quantity was another matter. A number of new construction techniques were used in the aircraft which made it more difficult to build than the earlier biplanes, and, in any case, the Supermarine factory was far too small to be able to handle a large production order. After considerable argument and repeated delays, with much of the work farmed out to subcontractors, the first production Spitfire (K9787) at last took to the air in the hands of Jeffrey Quill on May 15, 1938. It was powered by a Rolls-Royce Merlin II, which delivered its maximum 1,030 HP at 16,250 ft. Others followed slowly, but the first RAF unit to be equipped, Number 19 Squadron at Duxford, did not get its first Spitfire (K9789) until August 4. Even then, the early aircraft were far from being combat ready. Among the problems seeking solution, the engine starters were not powerful enough to guarantee a start, the unheated guns were prone to freezing up at high altitude, and the ailerons were found to be almost immovable at speeds above 400 MPH. Other improvements were needed, too. Tall pilots found the narrow canopy restricting, and the two-bladed, fixed-pitch, wooden propellers were able to make the most of the Merlin's power only at the higher end of the speed range.

Eventually, most of the difficulties were overcome. Stronger engine starters were fitted, hot air was ducted from the engine to the gun bays, metal ailerons aided high-speed maneuverability, the bulged Malcolm hood freed tall pilots from their cage, and three-bladed variable-pitch metal propellers improved the Spitfire's performance throughout the speed range.

Early shortcomings there might be, but the fighter's potential was obvious and inquiries were received from a number of countries. Japan, Belgium, Holland, Switzerland, Lithuania, Estonia, Yugoslavia, Greece, Turkey, Portugal, and France all expressed an interest in buying or building Spitfires. War intervened, however, and only one Spitfire was delivered overseas. It was flown to France for trials in June 1939 and eventually fell into German hands.

Operations Begin

It was not until the end of October 1938 that 19 Squadron was able to launch six aircraft at once for the official photographers, and it was December before the squadron had its full complement of sixteen Spitfires. From then on, the delivery rate increased slowly but steadily and, when war was declared on September 3, 1939, the RAF had received 306 Spitfires, enough to equip Numbers 19, 41, 54, 65, 66, 72, 74, 602, 603, and 611 Squadrons, with Number 609 Squadron building up. A great deal had been accomplished in a year, but, given what was known about the Luftwaffe, it was hardly enough.

It did not take long for the Spitfire to see action, but it was an inglorious beginning. On September 6, the "Battle of Barking Creek" was fought. A technical fault at a radar station led to reports of an enemy force approaching from the east, when the radar echoes were in fact from friendly aircraft to the west. Spitfires of 74 Squadron intercepted and attacked what they took to be enemy fighters over the Thames estuary and shot down two of them. Antiaircraft gunners engaged "enemy" twin-engined aircraft and destroyed one. When the fight was over, these "victories" were found to be two Hurricanes of 56 Squadron and a Blenheim of 64 Squadron. If there was a positive outcome to this disastrous encounter, it was that the production of IFF (Identification Friend or Foe) equipment for the RAF was given the highest priority.

Spitfires were not involved in action against the real enemy until October 16, 1939, when nine Junkers 88s of the Luftwaffe's KG30 appeared over the Firth of Forth near Edinburgh searching for Royal Navy warships. Squadron Leader Ernest Stevens, the commanding officer of Number 603 "City of Edinburgh" Squadron, led the attack on the bombers and became the first of

Spitfires from 19 Squadron in formation line abreast. Imperial War Museum

many RAF pilots to shoot down an enemy aircraft in British airspace during WWII. A second bomber was destroyed and a third seriously damaged as the raid was driven off.

Confrontations between the Spitfire and its Luftwaffe counterpart, the Messerschmitt Bf 109, began in May 1940, after Adolf Hitler had launched his assault in the west. Air Chief Marshal Sir Hugh Dowding, C-in-C Fighter Command, would not allow any of his precious Spitfire squadrons to be based outside Britain, so these first encounters took place near the outer edge of the Spitfire's radius of action, over Holland, Belgium, and France, and particularly during the evacuation of the British Army from Dunkirk. It was quickly apparent from these clashes that the rival fighters were fairly evenly matched. In level flight below 15,000 ft, the Spitfire I was margin-

Spitfires with flaps and undercarriage down come in to land. Imperial War Museum

Wing Commander A.C. Deere (right) with squadron mate.

The opening rounds of the Battle of Britain were fought in July 1940, and the struggle continued until the end of October. The German intention was to destroy RAF Fighter Command's capacity to defend British airspace, so clearing the way for an invasion of southern England. To accomplish that aim, the Luftwaffe had to inflict as much damage as possible on RAF airfields and radar stations, while fighting a battle of attrition with the RAF's fighter force. As the weeks went by, it became obvious that bomber formations had to be escorted by large numbers of Bf 109s for the Luftwaffe to have any hope of success. Good though it was, however, Messerschmitt's little fighter was not sufficiently overwhelming in numbers nor did it have the necessary edge in performance to allow it to achieve the desired air superiority over the Channel and southern England.

Al Deere, the indestructible New Zealander who flew the Spitfire and included three Bf 109s among his Battle of Britain victories, had no doubts about which was the superior aircraft. He wrote: "As a result of my prolonged fight with a 109, it was possible to assess the relative performance of the two aircraft. In early engagements...the speed and climb of the 109 had become legendary and were claimed by many to be far superior to the Spitfire. I was able to refute this contention and indeed was confident that, except in a dive, the Spitfire was superior in most fields and, like the Hurricane, vastly more maneuverable.... There were those who frankly disbelieved my claim, saying that it was contrary to published performance figures. Later events, however, proved me right."

Al Deere's opinion aside, at this stage of the war there were two features of the Bf 109's design which were noticeably better than the Spitfire's—armament and fuel supply. The widely spread rifle-caliber machine guns of the early Spitfires could not equal the hitting power of the 20 mm cannon and the centrally mounted machine guns of the Bf 109. In combat, too, it was discovered that the fuel-injected Daimler-Benz engine of the Bf 109 sometimes gave its pilot the opportunity to escape a pursuing Merlin-engined fighter. The Merlin's conventional carburetor could not cope with negative "G" maneuvers, and the engine cut out if negative G was applied. A hard-pressed Bf 109 could be pushed over under power into a dive, but, to follow, a Spitfire had to maintain positive G by being rolled on its back and pulled through. Quickly though that might

ally faster than the Bf 109E, but lost its speed advantage above that height. The Bf 109E accelerated the quicker and was a little better in the climb, but the Spitfire was the more maneuverable aircraft. Given that the differences were relatively slight, the outcome in any battle between the two usually depended more on other factors—opposing strengths, pilot ability, the position of the sun, height advantage, the tactics employed, etc.

The Battle of Britain

The early skirmishing over, the RAF and the Luftwaffe got ready for the main event.

Spitfire Mark IIA, Number 65 Squadron.

be done, the Bf 109 almost invariably gained a vital second or so. Given its better diving performance, that was sometimes enough to put the Bf 109 out of range of its pursuer.

When the Battle of Britain began, the number of Spitfire squadrons had risen to nineteen, with Numbers 64, 92, 152, 222, 234, 266, 610, and 616 re-equipping to join the original eleven. The Spitfires being delivered at this stage were not the same as the aircraft with which the RAF had started the war. Besides the improvements already mentioned, they were fitted with more armor plate to protect the pilot and the header tanks of the fuel and glycol systems. They were also using higher octane fuel, which made a significant difference to the Spitfire's low altitude performance, adding as much as 25 MPH to the maximum speed at sea level. This was just as well, since the all-up weight of the aircraft had risen by over 300 lbs, and various drag-producing items had been added, such as the IFF aerials and a toughened glass windscreen. When the beneficial and adverse factors were balanced out, the maximum speed of a Spitfire I in mid-1940 was about 350 MPH at 18,500 ft, compared to the trials figure of 362 MPH for the first production aircraft.

As the Battle of Britain reached its climax, the Spitfire Mk II began to appear, re-equipping Numbers 611, 19, 74, and 266 Squadrons during August and September. Externally, the Mk II differed very little from the Mk I, but it was powered by the slightly more powerful Merlin XII (1,140 HP at 14,750 ft), an engine which could be started by firing a cartridge. Some Mk IIs (and Mk Is) were fitted with two 20 mm cannon in the wings, but the experiment was not a success. (Cannon-armed Mk I and II Spitfires were designated IB and IIB; aircraft carrying only Browning machine guns were designated IA and IIA.) Much more work had to be done on the Hispano cannon, which suffered from continual stoppages, before it could be regarded as reliable. Number 19 Squadron's commander complained bitterly at having to take his cannon-armed Spitfires into battle, including in his report the remark: "It is most strongly urged that until the stoppages at present experienced have been eliminated this Squadron should be re-equipped with Browning gun Spitfires."

The Spitfire Mk II was built at a huge new Spitfire factory, at Castle Bromwich, near Birmingham. The most modern machine tools

Completed center sections of Spitfire aircraft.

available were used and the factory was managed by the car manufacturing company, Morris Motors Ltd. Eventually, the Castle Bromwich factory built more Spitfires than all other aircraft production facilities combined.

It was as well that the Castle Bromwich factory was up and running, and that the manufacturing of many Spitfire components had been subcontracted by September 1940. On September 26, the Luftwaffe effectively destroyed the Supermarine plants at Woolston and Itchen, near Southampton. Following the raid, more drastic measures were taken to ensure that Spitfire production was widely dispersed. Manufacturing premises were requisitioned in many parts of England, and machine tools were set up in large garages, commercial laundries, bus stations, and even a steamroller works.

With the coming of October, it became clear that the crisis of the Battle of Britain had been passed. Sporadic outbursts of activity occurred during the month, but the scale of the struggle steadily diminished. By the end of October the Luftwaffe had retired to lick its wounds and prepare for other things further east. Between July 10 and October 31, the RAF had lost 1,023 fighters and the Luftwaffe a total of 1,887 aircraft,

of which 873 were fighters. Almost thirty percent of the RAF's victories were credited to Spitfire squadrons, a proportion which approximated the number of Spitfires generally operating in the front line compared with other types. (Sixty-seven RAF fighter squadrons fought in the Battle of Britain, of which nineteen were equipped with Spitfires.)

High-speed Reconnaissance

As early as 1939, it was recognized that the solution to the problem of penetrating enemy airspace for the purposes of reconnaissance was a small, fast, high-flying aircraft which could sneak through (or over) defenses, take photographs, and return with minimal risk of interception. The Spitfire was proposed as the ideal answer, stripped of guns and armor, fitted with cameras, and loaded with as much fuel as it could carry.

Two Mk I Spitfires were modified as proposed into PR 1As and carefully finished to remove any surface blemishes, the final coat of paint being pale green. Early operations with the PR IAs were flown above 30,000 ft and penetrated Germany as far as Cologne. The results of these flights led to modifications which included cameras capable of recording much more detail, and

Clipped wing Spitfire Mark Vs.

an extra twenty-nine-gallon fuel tank behind the pilot. They were also painted a shade of blue which adorned most PR aircraft for the rest of the war. So modified, the aircraft became PR IBs, a medium-range version with a radius of action of 325 miles. The PR IC added underwing blisters which housed thirty gallons of fuel on one side and more cameras on the other. Later the PR ID (re-designated PR IV) carried first 114, then 133 gallons of fuel in the wing leading edge, together with fourteen extra gallons of oil to cover the longer sorties. The bulged cowling made to encompass this oil tank in the nose was distinctive. With this aircraft, Stettin was photographed on October 29, 1940, during a sortie which lasted for 5 hours and 20 minutes. Other variants were the PR IE (only one made), PR IF (an interim long-range version used until the PR IV could be introduced), and the PR IG. The IG was used for low-level reconnaissance, and, besides carrying sideways-looking cameras, it retained a fighter's eight-gun armament for self defense. IGs were painted a very pale shade of pink, which was deemed an appropriate color for low-level pen-etration. Losses in the units flying low-level reconnaissance were sometimes heavy. One of the pilots involved in covering German naval activi-ties, Gordon Green, has said:" During the early missions to cover Brest we lost about five pilots

fairly quickly. [Two new pilots] took off for Brest the evening they arrived, and neither came back. It was a very sobering incident."

The "Stopgap" Spitfire

The never ending demands for im-proved performance led initially to the Spitfire Mk III. For various reasons, however, the Mk III was overtaken by events, and only one was ever built. The Mk IV designation was allocated to the first of the Rolls-Royce Griffon Spitfires, but was then appropriated for the PR IV. The need seen as most pressing after the Battle of Britain was for improved high-altitude performance, to allow the Spitfire to fight effectively above 30,000 ft. A specially designed high-altitude version, the Mk VI, complete with pressure cabin, was on the drawing board, but it was still some way from production. The Mk VI did finally reach the front line in April 1942, but by then it, too, had been rendered largely superfluous by developments. The urgent need to meet the likely demands of aerial combat in 1941 drove the RAF to seek a stopgap, and the Mk V was devised. The first Mk Vs were converted Mk Is and IIs, strengthened to take the heavier and more powerful Merlin 45, a 1,440 HP engine with a single-speed supercharger.

The Mk V was initially produced in two forms—the VA, which had the standard eight

machine gun armament, and the VB, with two cannon and four machine guns. Later on, the VC appeared with the stronger "universal" wing, which could be fitted with either of the previous gun arrangements, or with four cannon. (By this time, the 20 mm cannon's stoppage problems had been cured.)

The first production Spitfire Vs were delivered to Number 92 Squadron at Biggin Hill in February 1941, and others followed in rapid succession. Almost all day fighter squadrons in Fighter Command had re-equipped with the Mk V by the end of 1941. With Hitler's turn to the east in 1941, the anticipated resumption of the Battle of Britain did not occur, and the RAF's fighter squadrons took on a more offensive role, carrying out repeated fighter sweeps over Ger-man-occupied Europe. For this, the Mk V was well suited, and it became the primary production version of the Spitfire, spawning a host of variants. By the time manufacture of the Mk V "stopgap" ceased, almost 6,500 had been built, and it went on to serve with no fewer than 117 RAF squad-rons.

To begin with, the Mk V gave RAF pilots a distinct edge over their Luftwaffe oppo-nents, but the advantage did not last. The Messerschmitt Bf 109F appeared later in the year, with a performance comparable to the Mk V, and soon thereafter the Focke-Wulf 190 was intro-duced. In a July 1942 trial between the Spitfire VB and a captured FW 190, it was found that, except in the radius of its turns, the German aircraft was the better fighter. In acceleration, rate of climb, maximum level and diving speeds, and rate of roll, the FW 190 was markedly superior to the Spitfire at all heights. It was perhaps fortunate for the RAF that in 1942 the Luftwaffe was heavily committed to the campaign against the Soviet Union and remained largely on the defensive in the west.

The first overseas deployment of Spit-fires took place in March 1942, when fifteen "tropicalized" Mk VBs were launched from the deck of HMS *Eagle* off the coast of Algiers to fly to Malta, which was under almost continuous attack from enemy bombers. To give them the necessary range, the VBs were fitted with ninety-gallon slipper tanks hung between the legs of the under-carriage. The tropical modification consisted of a large beard-like fairing under the nose which contained filters to protect the carburetor air intake from the dusty conditions of the Mediterranean theater. Other carrier deployments to Malta followed, including some from the USS *Wasp*, a much larger ship, capable of launching some fifty Spitfires in one operation.

The tropicalized Mk V's "beard" somewhat diminished the fighter's performance, but the Spitfire was nevertheless a formidable addition to the Allied effort in the Mediterranean. In this form, it featured in the November 1942 Allied invasion of North Africa, flown by the USAAF's 31st and 52nd Fighter Groups.

The American pilots were very fond of their Spitfires, and flew them throughout the campaigns in North Africa and Sicily, converting (not always willingly) to P-51 Mustangs in Italy during the spring of 1944. Bill Skinner of the 31st FG held a typical view of the Spitfire: "It was a fun plane to fly—there was nothing to worry about. It looked nice, it felt nice, it flew nice—it didn't take long before you felt comfortable in it." One of Skinner's fellow pilots in the 31st FG was Jerry Collinsworth, who became a Spitfire ace, shooting down six Luftwaffe aircraft, all of them FW 190s. He recalled his first meeting with a Spitfire after arriving in England: "I had never been close to a Spitfire before. It looked small and delicate, and when I gave the wing an experimental shake it seemed much too fragile to be a fighter. It was quite different in the air, however. Once the wheels were in the well, the Spitfire was all business. It was a wonderful combat aircraft." Besides those flown by the USAAF, 143 Spitfire VBs were supplied to the Soviet Air Force, delivered through Iran in 1943. Other foreign air forces later to receive Spitfire Vs included those of Turkey, Portugal, Italy, Yugoslavia, and Egypt. Mk Vs operated in every theater during WWII, first appearing in the Far East early in 1943, when Number 54 Squadron deployed to Darwin in the defense of Australia against Japanese bombing attacks.

During the Mk V's service life, it was subjected to all sorts of modifications, often aimed at improving performance for specific tasks. Those intended mainly for low-level roles (later known as the Spitfire LF V) had their wings clipped to increase the rate of roll, and to allow better acceleration and diving speed below 10,000 ft. The Merlin 50M engine used had a smaller supercharger, and gave 1,585 HP at 3,800 ft. Some Spitfire VCs had bomb racks fitted. A more general, and much welcomed, development was the introduction of a negative G carburetor for the

Mark V Spitfire with tropical air filter and a 250 lb bomb.   Imperial War Museum

USAAF 31st Fighter Group pilots scramble to their Spitfires.   Imperial War Museum

Spitfire Mark VII.   Imperial War Museum

Mark IX Spitfires over Italian beachheads.

Imperial War Museum

Merlin engine, which, in the words of the RAF trial report: "...transforms the Spitfire V into a much better fighting machine."

Another Hasty Adaptation

The appearance of the Focke-Wulf 190 before the end of 1941 led to a run of losses by Spitfire squadrons operating over the continent, and that soon disturbed the planned progression of the fighter's development. It had been intended that the next versions to reach the squadrons should be the Mk VII and the Mk VIII. The Spitfire VII was designed as a high-altitude fighter, with a strengthened airframe, retractable tail wheel, pressurized cockpit, and pointed wing tips which increased the wingspan from 36 ft 10 in to 40 ft 2 in. It was powered by a Merlin 61, with a two-stage supercharger. However, by the time it reached the front line in late 1942, the Mk VII did not offer significant advantages over other Spitfires and only 140 were built.

The Mk VIII was to have been the main production version, using the Mk VII's stronger airframe (without pressurization) and Merlin 61 engine, but with standard span wings. Unfortunately, the retooling required for production meant that the first Mk VIII could not be delivered earlier than the end of 1942, and, faced with the FW 190 threat, the RAF needed a Spitfire with boosted performance well before that. The answer was the Spitfire IX.

Two Spitfire VCs were quickly modified to take the 1,560 HP Merlin 61 and became the first Mk IXs. The trials of the new fighter were a revelation. The report concluded: "The performance of the Spitfire IX is outstandingly better than the Spitfire V, especially at heights above 20,000 ft. On the level the Spitfire IX is considerably faster and its climb is exceptionally good.... Its maneuverability is as good as the Spitfire V up to 30,000 ft, and above that is very much better. At 38,000 ft it is capable of a true speed of 368 MPH, and is still able to maneuver well for fighting." (At 28,000 ft, a true airspeed of 409 MPH was recorded.) Even better news followed in July 1942 when a fully operational Spitfire IX was tested against a captured FW 190. Although the FW 190 retained its rolling advantage over the Spitfire, and still had slightly better acceleration, the Mk IX proved to be faster than the German fighter at all heights, and could hold its adversary in the climb to 22,000 ft, at which height the Spitfire began pulling away. As many FW 190 pilots soon found out, the days of their unquestioned superiority were over. Spitfire IXs began arriving at RAF Hornchurch, near London, for Number 64 Squadron in June 1942, and other squadrons re-equipped rapidly in the months which followed. Number 133 "Eagle" Squadron got Mk IXs in August and September, and one of its American pilots recorded his impressions: "I made my first flight in [a Mk IX] on 26 August; she was a beauty. While the old Mk V became 'mushy' above 20,000 ft, the Mk IX with her more powerful Merlin and two-stage supercharger just seemed to go on and on up."

Among the particular threats tackled by the Spitfire IX was that of the very high-altitude bomber. In 1942, the Luftwaffe began launching single Junkers 86Rs over the UK. They flew above 40,000 ft and were invulnerable to interception. A special Spitfire IX unit was formed to deal with the problem, using aircraft stripped of armor and of all guns except two 20 mm cannon. On September 12, 1942, one of these special Spitfires, flown by Pilot Officer Prince Emanuel Galitzine, pursued a Ju 86R over Southampton. The bomber was caught and attacked at 43,000 ft, but the fighter's port gun jammed after firing the first burst. In subsequent attacks, the Spitfire slewed to starboard and fell away whenever the remaining gun fired. The Ju 86R therefore escaped, having been hit by only one shell. That was enough, however. Since it was clear that the bombers were no longer immune, the high-altitude raids were discontinued. (Plt. Off. Galitzine's engagement was the highest air battle of WWII.)

In more conventional operations, the Mk IX was a godsend to the fighter squadrons. "Johnnie" Johnson, the leading RAF ace to survive WWII, recorded his reaction to flying the new Spitfire: "...we were hardly crossing the French coast [with Spitfire Vs] because of the superiority of the FW 190. The Spitfire could turn inside the FW 190 but you can't turn forever.... [The Spitfire IX] was a big technical change. After fighting for the past year against the Focke-Wulf in the Spitfire V, I took a Spitfire IX off for the first time from Kenley, and someone asked me how I liked it. I said, *'I'm going to live! I'm bloody going to live now! We've got a machine that will see them off!'*"

Imperial War Museum

Group Captain "Johnny" Johnson.

Spitfire PR XI (photoreconnaissance).

As with the previous "stopgap" Spitfire, the Mk V, the Mk IX was produced in quantity and in various forms. The clipped-wing LF IX had the 1,720 HP Merlin 66; running on 150-octane fuel, its full throttle altitudes were 2,800 ft in the lower (MS) supercharger gear, and 13,800 ft in the higher (FS) gear. At the latter height, it had a maximum true airspeed of 389 MPH. HF IXs used the 1,710 HP Merlin 70, and had full-throttle heights of 14,600 ft in MS gear, and in FS 25,400 ft, where 405 MPH true airspeed was achieved. While that does not seem to give any advantage over a standard Mk IX, the HF IX was over five minutes quicker in getting to 36,000 ft, and its service ceiling, without modification, was more than 43,000 ft. Both the LF and HF IXs had fully loaded weights of about 7,400 lbs, over a ton more than the prototype K5054.

In the course of its development, the Spitfire IX absorbed numerous changes and improvements. Rear fuselage fuel tanks were added, and, eventually, teardrop canopies. Perhaps the most obvious alteration in the middle of the production run was to the shape of the tail. The familiar round-topped fin gave way to one with a broader chord and a pointed top. The standard wing for the Mk IX was different, too. It could be fitted with four 20 mm cannon, or with two cannon and four .5-in machine guns.

Finally, in 1944, supplies of the Merlin 266 were made available to the Castle Bromwich factory. The 266 was a low-altitude Merlin 66 manufactured under license by the Packard Motor Company in the United States. Although the Packard engine differed from its Rolls-Royce equivalent only slightly, the Spitfire IX airframes which received it were designated Mk XVIs. Some 5,656 Mk IXs and 1,054 Mk XVIs were built. Taken together with 280 Mk Vs converted to Mk IXs, the total number produced of this version of the Spitfire approached 7,000, making it the most numerous of the breed. Apart from seeing service with the RAF and USAAF, 1,188 of them were delivered to the Soviet Union, and many soldiered on well after the war in many other air forces including those of Norway, Denmark, Holland, Greece, Czechoslovakia, and Israel. Canadian, Australian, and New Zealand squadrons serving in the RAF generally took their aircraft home with them at the end of the war to form the core of their respective air forces.

Faster Photographers

The Spitfire IX's greatly improved performance led almost immediately to its adaptation for reconnaissance. Small numbers were modified for both the high- and low-altitude roles, and were known as PR IXs and FR IXs respectively. It was a PR IX of Number 542 Squadron which brought back photographs of the breached Möhne Dam after the famous low-level raid by Number 617 Squadron. Later, specialized reconnaissance Spitfires were built—PR Mks X, XI, and XIII. During its trials, the Mk XI recorded a maximum true airspeed of 417 MPH at 24,000 ft. The Spitfire airframe had become associated with high speeds, and some of the most remarkable were achieved in the dive, when the speed of sound was approached more closely than ever before. In the spring of 1944, a Spitfire PR XI was selected to carry out a series of dives to explore control problems at high Mach numbers. On April 27, 1944, "Marty" Martindale had reached Mach 0.89 (TAS 606 MPH) when: "...there was a fearful explosion and the aircraft became enveloped in white smoke.... The aircraft shook from end to end." After discovering that the aircraft was still flying, and that chinks had appeared in an initially complete

From left, Group Captain A.G. Malan (South Africa), Squadron Leader Jack Charles (Canada), and Wing Commander A.C. Deere (New Zealand).

oil film over the canopy, Martindale turned towards base. A forced landing seemed inevitable, since, as he said: "The engine was clearly not going and I could see no propeller. Bits of engine were sticking out and the engine appeared to have shifted sideways." Martindale completed a successful wheels down forced landing at Farnborough, and then found that the entire propeller and reduction gear had broken away, a connecting rod had pushed its way out of the crankcase, and a main engine bearer was buckled. As if that were not enough, Martindale suffered a repeat performance the following month, when a supercharger burst at 600 MPH and the engine caught fire. This time, he was not so fortunate. The Spitfire crashed into a wood, Martindale escaping with spinal injuries and earning the subsequent award of the Air Force Cross.

A number of PR XIs were supplied to the USAAF and were used to carry out post-attack reconnaissance for the 8th Air Force. Although the Supermarine fighter was notorious for its short range, as a PR aircraft it could exhibit a surprisingly long reach. In March 1944, for example, a PR XI of the USAAF's 7th Reconnaissance Group flew from England to Berlin to photograph the results of the previous day's raid on the German capital, staying airborne 4 hours and 18 minutes in the process. At one point, a challenge was made on the high-flying Spitfire by three specially modified Bf 109s. When he saw them closing on him from behind, the pilot, Walt Weitner, resisted the temptation to drop his slipper tank, and then: "...pushed the throttle forward as far as it would go without selecting emergency power, eased the nose up and began to climb. At 41,500 ft I leveled off and my indicated airspeed increased to 178 MPH (about 360 MPH true). After what seemed forever, but was probably only two to three minutes, the German fighters began to fall back and slid out of sight. Had they come any closer, I would have gone to emergency boost, but it never got that desperate."

Merlin Spitfire Perfection

In due course, the necessary preparatory work was completed for the production of the Spitfire VIII, and it replaced the Mk IX as the version built by the Supermarine factories. Castle Bromwich continued with the Mk IX. In essence, there was little to choose between the performance of the two versions. Nevertheless, some experienced pilots preferred the VIII. Jeffrey

Spitfire Mark XIV.

Quill, Supermarine's Chief Test Pilot, has said: "When I am asked which mark of Spitfire I consider the best from the pure flying point of view, I usually reply 'The Mk VIII with standard wing-tips.'" One thousand six hundred fifty-eight Spitfire VIIIs were built. They equipped some thirty squadrons and were used extensively in the Mediterranean and the Far East.

The Coming of the Griffon

Successful, adaptive, and long-lasting though the Merlin proved to be, the Rolls-Royce engineers knew that eventually more power would be needed than the 27-liter Merlin could be induced to supply. At an early stage of WWII, work was begun on a new twelve-cylinder engine, named the Griffon, based on the Merlin but with a capacity of 36.7 liters. Clever design kept the Griffon's frontal area to within six percent of the Merlin's, while it grew just three inches in length and only 600 lbs in weight.

The most confusing aspect of the Griffon Spitfire's history is the juggling of Mark numbers which bedeviled the first examples. The airframe selected for the first Griffon was the Mk III, which became a Mk IV when fitted with a Griffon IIB. This was changed to Mk XX to avoid confusion with the PR IV. For some obscure reason, this was later changed again to Mk XII. As part of the effort to counter the FW 190 in 1942—especially the FW 190A fighter-bombers

making nuisance attacks along England's south coast—the Spitfire XII was ordered into production, and the aircraft began reaching squadrons in February 1943. In trials, the Mk XII had shown conclusively that it was faster than the FW 190 and the Hawker Typhoon at low altitude, and in 1944 it proved useful in being able to catch and shoot down V-1 flying bombs directed against London. Fast as it was at low level, however, the Spitfire XII was inferior to Merlin Spitfires at higher altitude. This was because it had been hurried into production with early-model Griffons, fitted with single-stage superchargers. By 1943, two-stage supercharging was available, and the Griffon 61 appeared. Six Mk VIIIs were converted to take this engine, and they served as prototypes for the Spitfire XIV. The most obvious identifying external features of the Griffon-powered aircraft were the longer nose and the bulges in the previously smooth outline of the cowling to accommodate the larger engine, the deeper radiator ducts under both wings, and the much more prominent spinner housing the roots of what was usually a five-bladed propeller. Another quirky difference between the Griffon-powered aircraft and the Merlin Spitfires was that Rolls-Royce had made the Griffon rotate the opposite way from its predecessor. Unwary Spitfire pilots, used to Merlins, could be surprised by the Griffon fighter's determined move to the right instead of left during takeoff.

Spitfire Mark 22.

The first production Spitfire XIVs were delivered towards the end of 1943 and they began arriving on squadrons at the beginning of 1944. They were fitted with the 2,050 HP Griffon 65, and their improvement in performance over the Spitfire IX was as great as had been that fighter's advance over the Mk V. Maximum true airspeeds reached were 391 MPH at 5,000 ft and 448 MPH at 26,000 ft. The service ceiling was 44,500 ft. Following comparative trials against the Spitfire IX, Tempest V, Mustang, FW 190, and Bf 109G, it was concluded that: "[The Spitfire XIV] has the best all-round performance of any present-day fighter, apart from range."

The Spitfire XIV was one of WWII's fastest fighters and proved its worth repeatedly against the V-1 flying bombs in 1944. It was also the first RAF aircraft to shoot down a Messerschmitt 262 jet fighter. Nine hundred fifty-seven Mk XIVs were built, many equipping squadrons based in the Far East during the latter stages of the war. When the Royal Auxiliary Air Force was reformed in 1946, the Spitfire XIV temporarily became its standard day fighter; Number 612 "County of Aberdeen" Squadron kept its Spitfires until July 1951. Other Mk XIVs found their postwar way to the air forces of Belgium, India, and Thailand.

Both the Mk XIV and its almost identical cousin, the Mk XVIII, were produced in fighter and fighter/reconnaissance versions. The FR variants carried cameras mounted in the rear fuselage. Spitfire XVIIIs, essentially upgraded and strengthened Mk XIVs, entered service too late to fight in WWII, but saw some action in the 1950s during the Malayan emergency. It was the Mk XVIII's distinction to be the last Spitfire to fly with the purely elliptical wing developed by Reginald Mitchell.

The Spitfire PR XIX had appeared more than a year before the Mk 18. (Arabic numerals usually replaced Roman numerals for Spitfire designations from Mk 21 onwards, and for the Mk 18 after 1945.) It was a reconnaissance aircraft of extraordinary capabilities, combining the fuel tanks and cameras of the Mk XI with the Griffon engine of the Mk XIV and the pressure cabin of the Mk X. It cruised comfortably at 40,000 ft at 370 MPH, and in postwar exercises it often reached 49,000 ft on its approach to targets. Not until the introduction of the MiG-15 and F-86 were there fighters which could challenge the PR XIX with any prospect of achieving an interception.

All Good Things Come to an End

When the Rolls-Royce Griffon first became a practical proposition, the Supermarine design team, led by Joseph Smith, recognized that, to take advantage of the full potential of the engine, a major redesign of the Spitfire airframe would be necessary. The proposed aircraft was given the designation Mk 21. It grew into a much stronger machine than its predecessors, with stiffened wings, a wider stance undercarriage, and longer legs to create ground clearance for a five-bladed propeller of 11 ft diameter. Most notably, it was fitted with ailerons which were five percent larger than any used before, and these brought about the first change in the basic shape of the Spitfire's wing since the prototype.

Great things were expected of the Mk 21, and orders were placed for some 3,000. However, the initial reaction to the new fighter when it appeared was not encouraging. Trials flown at the end of 1944 resulted in a report which said that in certain circumstances the aircraft was: "...almost dangerous to fly," and included the unexpected recommendation that: "...the Spitfire

A pilot climbs into his Spitfire Mark 18 during the Malayan emergency, c. 1950.

21 be withdrawn from operations until the instability in the yawing plane has been removed...." It then went further and came to the shocking conclusion that: "...in its present state it is not likely to prove a satisfactory fighter. No further attempts should be made to perpetuate the Spitfire family." The alarm provoked by the trials report was premature, but it took much burning of midnight oil at Supermarine to correct the problems. A number of modifications were devised and, by March 1945, the Mk 21 was no longer causing anxiety, although it remained the most difficult and least pleasant of all Spitfires to fly. In any event, the end of the war overtook production and only 120 Spitfire 21s were built. During its brief fighting life, the Mk 21 did score one unusual combat success; on April 26, 1945, two Mk 21s caught a midget submarine on the surface off The Hook of Holland and claimed it as sunk by cannon fire.

The Spitfire 22 differed from the Mk 21 in having the cut-back rear fuselage and teardrop canopy as standard. In the production version, it also featured a larger tail, which significantly improved the handling characteristics. Only 278 Mk 22s were built, and the fighter was operated by only one regular RAF squadron, Number 73 in the Middle East. Most went to the Royal Auxiliary Air Force, and others to the air forces of Southern Rhodesia, Egypt, and Syria.

The last of the Spitfires, the Mk 24, was little more than a modified Mk 22. It carried more fuel and was fitted both with a short-barrel version of the 20 mm cannon and with rocket launchers. Only 54 were built, and a further 27 were converted Mk 22s. The only RAF unit to operate the

Mk 24 was Number 80 Squadron, first from Gütersloh in Germany, and later from Hong Kong. Spitfire 24s remained in service with the Hong Kong Auxiliary Air Force until 1955.

Reginald Mitchell's inspired design had stood the test of time and had absorbed all the growth demanded of it. When it first flew in 1935, it had legitimate claims to being the finest fighter in the world, and, with the delivery of the last Mk 24 in 1948, it still stood in the front rank of piston-engined fighters. It is revealing to compare the figures for the first and last of the operational Spitfires:

	Spitfire I	
	Spitfire 24	
Loaded weight	5,935 lbs	
	10,100 lbs	
Fuel capacity	84 gallons	
	186 gallons	
Power	RR Merlin II; 1,030 HP	
	RR Griffon 85; 2,050 HP	
Max speed	355 MPH at 19,000 ft	
	454 MPH at 26,000 ft	
Rate of climb	30,000 ft in 16½ min	
	30,000 ft in 9 min	
Service ceiling	34,000 ft	
	43,000 ft	
Range	500 miles	
	580 miles	
Armament	8 x .303 machine guns	
	4 x 20 mm cannon; rockets	

Variations on a Theme Sublime

Throughout its life, the Spitfire proved to be amenable to adaptation, and there were many ideas proposed for its employment beyond

those which became mainstream developments. One of the earliest was the "Speed Spitfire," a stripped Mk 1 with a high-speed blue and silver finish and smoothed-out cockpit line, intended for a 1939 bid to capture the world landplane speed record. A sprint Merlin, capable of producing over 2,000 HP for short periods, was to be used. Trials were flown and the aircraft reached 408 MPH at 3,000 ft, but the project died when Germany stole the show with runs of 463 MPH by the Heinkel 100 and then 469 MPH by the Messerschmitt 209. The onset of war saw the Speed Spitfire retired to the role of "high-speed hack," and it served as such until being scrapped in 1946.

A number of Spitfires were fitted with contrarotating propellers in attempts to make the most of the power available, and to take care of problems associated with engine torque and the gyroscopic effects of a single propeller. At least five Mk IXs with the Merlin 77, and several Griffon-engined Marks flew with Rotol contrarotating propellers at one time or another. Almost invariably, the trials reports were enthusiastic, stressing the advantages of freedom from skid and slip in flight. The propellers were not adopted for production aircraft, however, because at the time of the trials they were not thought sufficiently reliable for general service use and they were undeniably heavy.

Other trials were flown with Spitfires on floats and on skis, and several alternative methods of increasing the aircraft's ferry range were tried. Besides a variety of conventional overload tanks, there was the Malinowski Trailer idea, which consisted of a large airfoil section tank towed behind a Spitfire on booms attached on each side at midwing. Interesting though it was, it never reached beyond the drawing board. Perhaps even more startling was the scheme which proposed towing the Spitfire, engine shut down, behind a larger aircraft. Tests were flown, towing a Mk IX behind a Wellington bomber, but the strain on the Spitfire pilot of continually wrestling with his aircraft behind the tug was such that the system was abandoned as impractical.

For much of the Spitfire's career, no requirement was seen for a two-seat trainer. Young RAF pilots generally had little difficulty in converting directly from the Harvard to the Spitfire. Local modifications were carried out during WWII in the Middle East, by Number 261 Squadron, and in the Soviet Union, where a number of Mk

Spitfire Mark IX experimental floatplane, taking off.   Imperial War Museum

Spitfire Mark VIII trainer.

IXs were modified as trainers. Postwar, Supermarine engineered a more ambitious conversion of a Mk VIII, which involved moving the normal cockpit forward 13½ in and adding a raised cockpit immediately behind. The RAF was not interested in the Spitfire trainer, but orders were placed by several other air forces, including those of India, Ireland, Holland, and Egypt.

All at Sea

The Spitfire story would not be complete without a brief mention of the navalized version of the aircraft—the Seafire. Generally, these Fleet Air Arm fighters bore close resemblance to their RAF counterparts, with the obvious addition of modifications required for life aboard ship. In the early part of WWII, the Royal Navy's capacity for air defense was unimpressive, consisting of such outdated aircraft as the Sea Gladiator, the Skua, and the Fulmar, none of them capable of reaching 250 MPH. To fill the gap, some Wildcats (known as Martlets) were acquired from the U.S., but the longer-term solution was clearly going to be a fighter based on the Spitfire.

The first Spitfires to reach the Navy early in 1942 were converted Mk VBs. The navalization process included the addition of suitable radios, arrester hooks, and slinging points. Designated Seafire IBs, there were 166 of them,

used largely for shore station training purposes. Three hundred seventy-two Seafire IICs (converted Mk VCs) followed and began arriving with operational squadrons in September 1942. Number 885 Squadron embarked in HMS *Formidable* in October and were involved in covering the Allied landings in North Africa in November.

The Seafire III, provided with the increased power of a 1,585 HP Merlin 55, took the naval conversion one logical stage further by adding folding wings. At this stage, the folding process, which broke each wing in two places, was a manual one, requiring a team of five men, but it did save valuable space on board ship. Seafire IIIs became operational with Number 894 Squadron in November 1943. The following May, together with the Seafires of Number 887 Squadron in HMS *Indefatigable*, they provided cover for air attacks on the German battleship *Tirpitz* in Norway's fjords.

The Mk XV was the first of the Griffon-powered Seafires. This Mark introduced a new sting type of arrester hook, secured to a single point and replacing the old A-frame mounting on earlier aircraft. The Mk XV did not see wartime service, however, and did not arrive with squadrons until 1947. Produced in parallel was the Seafire XVII, with a greatly improved twenty-four-volt electrical system and a much stronger undercarriage, more resistant to the punishment of repeated deck landings. The last three Seafires

were the Mks 45, 46, and 47, which were generally equivalent to the Spitfire 21, 22, and 24. Most Seafire 47s were fitted with contrarotating propellers, and were impressive performers—maximum speed 452 MPH at 20,500 ft; 4 min 50 sec to 20,000 ft; service ceiling above 43,000 ft. The last Seafire 47 squadron, Number 800, saw action in the opening phase of the Korean War before disbanding in November 1950.

Afterlife

The Spitfire was much too good an aircraft to let die, or even to fade away. The sight and sound of Mitchell's beautiful and potent design have so much power to stir the blood and conjure up past glories. It is hardly surprising to find that, more than sixty years after the prototype's first flight, the Royal Air Force still operates several Spitfires, both Merlin and Griffon. The aircraft of the Battle of Britain Memorial Flight serve as a constant reminder of the RAF's principal battle honor and of the vital role played by the service in defense of the UK.

It is no great wonder, either, that so many private individuals and museums have sought to own a Spitfire, or that the survivors of the breed are tended by their owners with such loving care. Spitfires seen on the ground at air shows draw a crowd and rightly so, but it is in the air that the true magic of the Spitfire is revealed. The slim, elegant lines and the educated snarl are unique, and those lucky enough to fly a Spitfire usually find that their stock of superlatives is inadequate to do justice to the experience. Ervin Miller flew Spitfires with Number 133 "Eagle" Squadron and with the 336th Fighter Squadron, 4th Fighter Group, USAAF. His memories are typical of those recalled by the fortunate few who were Spitfire pilots: "Even now, many years after I flew them on operations, the mere sound or sight of a Spitfire brings me a deep feeling of nostalgia and many pleasant memories. She was such a gentle little airplane, without a trace of viciousness. She was a dream to handle in the air. I feel genuinely sorry for the modern fighter pilot who has never had a chance to get his hands on a Spitfire. He will never know what real flying is like."

Previous page: The Spitfire Mk IIA P7350 from the RAF Battle of Britain Memorial Flight. This is the oldest airworthy Spitfire in the world. It saw action during the Battle of Britain, survived the war in gunnery school roles, and was on static display until restored to flying condition in 1967 for the movie, The Battle of Britain. The earliest Spitfires carried a two-bladed wooden fixed-pitch propeller. The next generation was fitted with a three-bladed variable-pitch prop as seen here.

The Spitfire Mk IIA shows the distinctive characteristics that were to stay with the fighter through its evolution. The side door hinged from the bottom and allowed easier entry into the rather snug cockpit. It could also be lowered for a pilot to bail out in the event that combat damage made the fighter unflyable. The "Malcom" hood, a blown Perspex canopy, allowed for much greater visibility than the ribbed greenhouse canopies characteristic of fighters like the Hurricane. A number of American fighters were converted to this type of canopy when the U.S. entered the war.

The Mk IIA fighter seen from the front quarter. The three-bladed propeller, while an advance from earlier versions, was still made of wood. In the case of a forced landing or the need to belly the airplane onto the ground, a wooden prop would shatter and allow the engine to turn RPM, avoiding the more serious damage that could be caused by an immediate engine stop.

Following page: The Spitfire Mk IX represents the evolution of the fighter to meet the ever changing threat from the Luftwaffe. This version carries a much more powerful engine and heavier armaments for aerial combat. The Spitfire's signature elliptical wings are visible in this photograph, as well as the four-bladed propeller needed to transfer the additional engine power into usable thrust.

The Spitfire was built with a narrow undercarriage, similar in appearance to the Messerschmitt Bf 109, although the Spitfire was not as susceptible to ground operation accidents. The fighter was designed to be used off rough fields as well as hard surface runways. During the Battle of Britain, fighter squadrons operated from nearly unimproved fields close to the coast so they could respond to the Luftwaffe threat as quickly as possible. The panels that cowl the engine can be seen at upper right. Dzus fasteners hold the panels in place at the speeds needed to dogfight but could be removed with a quarter turn.

A

B

A   The tail plane of the Mk IIA. One of the liabilities of the early Spitfires was the small rudder surface. At times, the rudder became ineffective, particularly on landing, as airspeed dropped off and the pilot approached the runway, making crosswind landings an adventure. One advantage to operating from a grass station was the ability to land into the wind, an option not always possible with a hard surface runway. The fighter is painted in the markings of 72 Squadron, the distinctive RAF "fin flash" on the vertical stabilizer.

B   The trim tab on the horizontal stabilizer allows the pilot to trim the fighter for the flight attitude necessary for the mission he is performing: straight and level for long flights, or slightly nose up or nose down depending on the responsiveness required. Trim also changes as the fuel carried on board is consumed and the weight and balance of the airplane vary. During WWII, pilots discovered that in high speed dives, the trim tabs were all that could be moved to pull out, as the elevators became frozen by the airspeed. The trim tabs brought the nose of the fighter up just enough to regain control.

A

B

A   *The tail of the Spitfire Mk IIA carries the camouflage and RAF fin flash from the Battle of Britain. The dark earth and green paint are symbolic of the fight over the fields of the UK.*

B   *The tail of the Spitfire Mk VB still has the early, smaller rudder. It is painted in the gray and green camouflage of later in the war, and the RAF fin flash now has much less white to subdue the image.*

C   *The larger rudder of the tail of the Spitfire Mk IX illustrates the evolution of the fighter. The larger rudder accommodates increased engine power and offers pilots greater rudder authority in combat and during critical takeoff and landing.*

D   *The tail of a Spitfire Mk XIX, with even larger rudder area, shows the continued progression of the airplane. This fighter is painted in a special shade called "PR blue," a color that was created for the high flying photoreconnaissance Spitfires that flew unarmed at altitudes above 40,000 feet.*

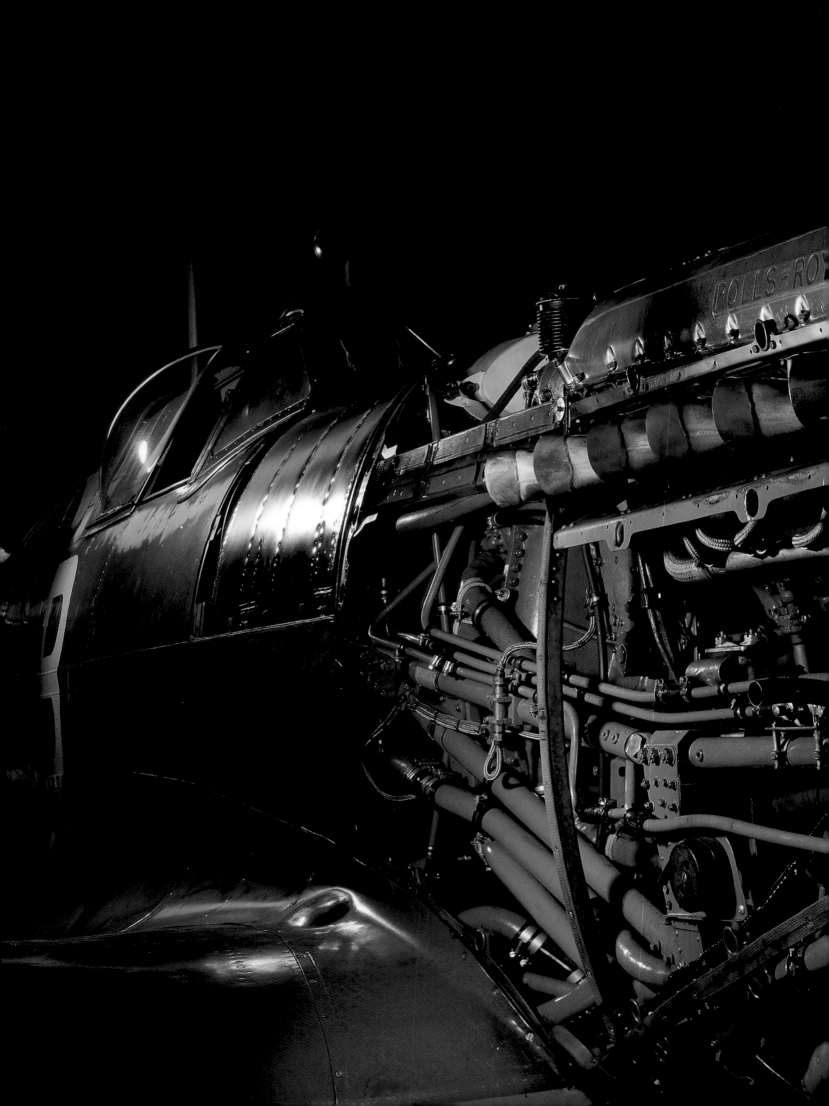

A

Previous page: The Rolls-Royce Merlin engine, the heart of the Spitfire, and also a part of the continuing evolution of the fighter as it was changed to answer the technological needs of aerial combat. This Mk IX fighter is owned and operated by The Old Flying Machine Company at Duxford, England. The Mk IX carried a Merlin engine that delivered 1,710 horsepower through a four-bladed Rotol propeller. The engine is uncowled here with the spinner removed from the propeller hub.

A   The Mk V, running up. Beneath the wings, aft of the undercarriage wells, is the oil cooler inlet. On the center line of the belly is the air intake for the engine.

B   On the Mk IX, the oil coolers have become much larger, reflecting the increased engine size, power, and the associated need for more efficient transmission of the engine's heat. Spitfires, as well as other fighters powered by liquid cooled engines, were very susceptible to any damage of the cooling system. There is a finite amount of time a Merlin engine will run with a leak in the cooling system before the pilot needs to be on the ground or looking for a place to bail out.

B

A   *The exhaust stubs of the twelve-cylinder Merlin.*

B   *When the cowling panels are removed, the complex plumbing that keeps the engine running becomes visible.*

C   *The carefully designed oil tank for the engine fits "just so" under the engine and inside the panels, allowing for the elegant streamlined shape of the Spitfire.*

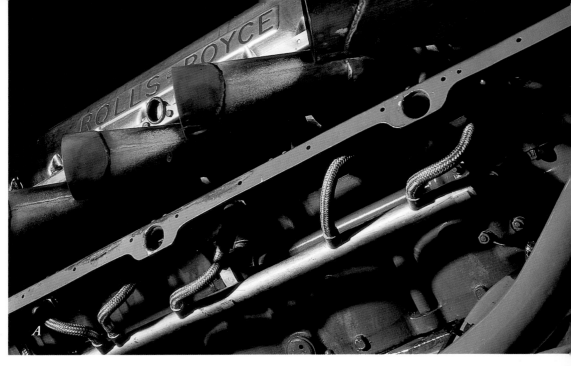

A   *Another Spitfire evolution was the size and weight of armaments. The Mk IIA shown here was armed with eight .303-caliber machine guns. The rifle-caliber guns proved ineffective against opposing aircraft and of no use in trying to disable an airplane engine. The gun ports here are covered with the red tape used by fitters to show the pilot that his guns had been serviced and rearmed. A quick look by the pilot when being "scrambled" to meet a challenge told him that his guns were ready for combat.*

B   *The Mk VB had 20 mm cannons added to its wings. The long barrels of the Hispano-Suiza cannon are seen inboard of the .303 machine guns under the red tape. The 20 mm cannon shells were devastating to an aircraft, fatal to a pilot, and could destroy an engine.*

C   *The muzzle of the 20 mm cannon on the Spitfire Mk VB.*

A

A   On the Mk IX, the long cannon barrels were enclosed inside a streamlined fairing. During the pilot's preflight, he always needed to check the guns to confirm that they were loaded, since his survival depended on it.

B   A comparison of Allied aircraft shells. From top: British .303 rifle-caliber bullet, U.S. .50-caliber standard machine gun bullet, and a 20 mm cannon shell.

B

A   The cockpit of the Spitfire Mk IIA with the flight instruments directly in front of the pilot. Inside the rectangle, on the top row, from the left: the airspeed indicator, artificial horizon, and rate-of-climb indicator. Bottom row, from the left: altimeter, gyroscopic compass, and turn indicator. To the right of the panel are the instruments to monitor engine performance. Directly below the panel is the compass, and between the compass and the seat is the control stick.

B   Looking into the cockpit from the wing, the pilot's seat is attached to the airframe by rails. Behind the seat is steel plate to protect the pilot from attacks from the rear. The well worn headrest is covered with leather.

A The distinctive "spade" grip of the pilot's control stick. The firing button for the guns is on the upper left of the grip. Different from most American fighters, where the pilot moves the entire stick forward and back for diving and climbing and side to side for banking, the Spitfire's pilot moves the spade grip side to side to bank the fighter, while still moving the entire stick forward and back to change pitch.

B At the pilot's left are the engine controls.

C RAF airplanes all carry a compass that looks like it would be at home in a warship, floating flat in a pool of oil.

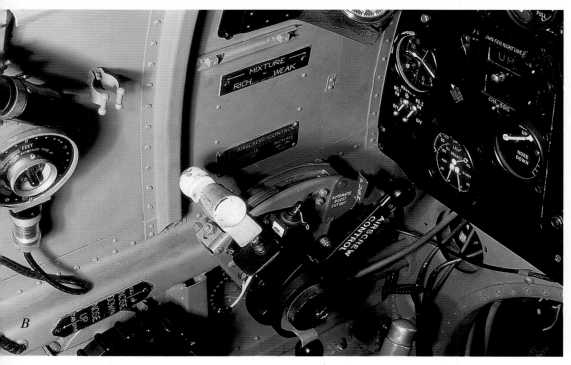

A   An early addition to the pilot's equipment was a rearview mirror. The Spitfire, until the very late versions, had poor visibility to the rear, or six o'clock position, which was an often fatal location to have a blind spot. To the right of the mirror along the front canopy rib is the heavy armored glass of the windscreen.

B   The pilot's hands are busy flying a single-seat fighter, the left hand on the engine controls and the right hand flying the airplane. The pilot of a Spitfire also had to be navigator and flight engineer. When carrying ordnance, he was also the bombardier.

C   The inside of the access door of the Spitfire with the red crowbar in its clip. If the pilot was trapped inside his fighter because the canopy was jammed or the door stuck, he could use the crowbar to bash his way out.

Before every mission, the fighter pilot does a "walk-around" inspection of his aircraft. While the RAF's ground crews are legendary for their efficiency and attention to details, the pilot must also be confident that his airplane is fully prepared to fly and fight.

A   Visual inspection of the propeller and the spinner is crucial. Any imperfections in the prop can lead to disaster at combat speeds.

B   The simple act of running a hand over the surface of a fighter can reveal a potential problem, such as a fluid leak or a loose panel.

C   The walk-around inspection includes checking, by hand, that all movable control surfaces are free and clear of any obstructions.

C

Imperial War Museum

50

A   Before putting on his parachute and flight helmet, the pilot checks the movement of the elevator. He is wearing a yellow life preserver, required for overwater flights.

B   The cumbersome parachute and flight equipment are the last things to don before climbing into the fighter.

C   Assisted by the ground crew, the pilot climbs into the fighter. Even with the access door open, it is still a chore to get into the cockpit.

D   The strength of the rearview mirror structure is apparent; the pilot uses it to steady himself as he lowers into the seat.

E   Strapped in and ready to go, the pilot is now alone, dependent only on the Spitfire, himself, and his skills to fly the mission.

A

A   The Mk VB taxis along the grass.

B   The Rolls-Royce engine of the Mk IX comes to life.

A

A   The Merlin engine requires a careful warm-up before taking the runway. When the critical temperatures are reached, takeoff needs to be fairly quick, as the closely cowled engine can rapidly begin to overheat.

B   With the Rolls-Royce Merlin engine at takeoff power, the Spitfire Mk IX roars off the grass runway at Audley End.

C   When the pilot has safely left the ground, the undercarriage retract outward into the wheel wells.

D   Making a low pass, the Mk IX displays the classic lines of the famous British fighter. The black and white stripes on the wings and fuselage were painted on Allied aircraft the night before the D-Day invasion of June 6, 1944, for easy identification from the ground.

Following page: The Mk IX flies offshore over the Kent coast and the English Channel.

B

C

D

A

A *This photograph emphasizes the sleek design of the Spitfire as it flies over the English Channel. The red, white, and blue circle under the cockpit is the marking of Number 312 Squadron, flown by Czech pilots.*

B *Turning away from the sun, a fighter pilot always has to be aware of his position, as the enemy has an advantage attacking from the sun.*

Following page: The Spitfire Mk IX flies over the Kent countryside, a decidedly welcome sight during the early 1940s.

B

Against the deep blue of the English Channel, the Spitfire pulls up and banks away.

Acknowledgments

The photographs done for this book would not have been possible without the considerable help of the following individuals and organizations:

Clive Denney, Historic Flying Limited. Clive's infectious enthusiasm made it possible to shoot the air-to-air photographs of the Spitfire Mk IX for this book. Spitfire TE566 is from the Historic Flying Collection, owners Guy Black and Angus Spence-Nairn. Their permission to photograph their rare fighter helped make this project come to life. Historic Flying Ltd. is a premier restoration facility for Spitfires and other World War II aircraft. Hidden away along the grass strip at Audley End, Clive and the craftsmen and women who work there are essentially building new airplanes out of the hulks they start with. Linda Denney and their sons, Glenn and Andrew, made me feel at home.

Martin Sergeant, Goudhurst, Kent, UK. Martin flies an immaculate North American Harvard, G-BGOR, from his grass strip. His specialty, among many talents, is the restoration and maintenance of Bentley and Rolls-Royce automobiles. Martin and I experienced the unique thrill of flying in formation with two famous fighters over the Battle of Britain Memorial near Folkstone on the weekend that commemorates the battle.

Squadron Leader Paul Day, Officer Commanding, RAF, Battle of Britain Memorial Flight, RAF Coningsby. Squadron Leader Day opened the doors to the BBMF and the collection of living, breathing World War II airplanes. Their stable of fighters includes the oldest airworthy Spitfire. I was treated as a VIP while visiting the BBMF, a unique experience for a photographer from Ohio.

Mark Hanna and his talented team of mechanics: Roger Shepherd, Chief Engineer; Martin Thompson; Tim Fane; and Ray Caller from The Old Flying Machine Company, Duxford. Mark also let me use the office as a home base for operations while I was in the UK, and I appreciate the hospitality.

David Henchie, Airfield Manager at Duxford.

Paul French, London. Paul and his wife Lydia adjusted their schedule and drove to Audley End on a Sunday for Paul to become the pilot for the photographs in this book. Paul also made the supreme sacrifice and shaved his beard for this project.

Glenn Denney and Anthony Bayfield also assisted in the photographs by becoming ground crewmen in the photographs.

Kurt Weidner, Dayton, Ohio. Kurt's knowledge of RAF artifacts is vast and his friendship is true. The still life at the front of this book represents just part of his collection.

My kids, Nate, Brigitta, and Joe. Also my parents, Bill and Jane Patterson, for helping me with the kids when I am chasing airplanes as well as for their ongoing support.

Ross and Elinor Howell, Howell Press. Ross continues to believe in and support what I do and how I do it.

Ron Dick, my compatriot, friend, and partner. We keep finding things to do books about.

Cheryl Terrill, for an understanding friendship.

I would also like to thank the following for helping to make this book possible: David Farnsworth, Jeffrey Ethell, David Hake, Tom Whalen, and Paul Perkins.

Technical Notes

The original photography in this book was all done with the intent to as faithfully as possible remove the clues of the present day and try to look back through a window opened by the owners and operators of these aircraft, a window into the 1940s when formations of these airplanes flew over the European continent during World War II.

I used a variety of cameras and equipment to complete this project: a Wista 4x5 Field View camera with a 150mm Caltar II lens and a 90mm Nikkor lens; a Mamiya RB67 with 50mm, 90mm, and 180mm lenses; a Nikon F3 with a motor drive and a Nikon 8008 with a garden variety of Nikkor lenses.

All the photographs were shot as transparencies to make the best possible color separations.

The 4x5 and 6x7 photos were all shot on Kodak Ektachrome Daylight film. The 35mm photos were taken with Ektachrome Lumiere.

The concept, design, and the photographs are done by Dan Patterson, 6825 Peters Pike, Dayton, Ohio 45414.

Bibliography

Armitage, Michael. *The Royal Air Force—
an Illustrated History*. London: Arms &
Armour Press, 1993.

Deere, Alan C. *Nine Lives*. London: Hodder &
Stoughton, 1959.

Deighton, Len and Max Hastings. *Battle of
Britain*. London: Michael Joseph, 1990.

Dorr, Robert F. and David Donald. *Fighters of the
USAF*. New York: Military Press, 1990.

Galland, Adolf. *The First and the Last*. London:
Methuen, 1955.

Green, William and Gordon Swanborough. *The
Complete Book of Fighters*. New York:
Smithmark, 1994.

Grinsell, Robert, Bill Sweetman, et al. *The Great
Book of WW2 Airplanes*. New York:
Bonanza Books, 1984.

Gunston, Bill. *British Fighters of World War II*.
New York: Crescent Books, 1982.

Halley, James J. *The Squadrons of the Royal Air
Force*. UK: Air-Britain
Publications, 1980.

Jablonski, Edward. *Air War*. New York:
Doubleday, 1979.

Mason, Francis K. *The British Fighter since 1912*.
London: Putnam, 1992.

Mason, Frank. *Battle over Britain*. London:
McWhirter Twins, 1969.

Price, Alfred. *The Hardest Day*. London:
MacDonald & Jane's, 1979.

_____. *Spitfire at War*. London: Ian Allan
Publishing, 1974.

_____. *Spitfire at War 2*. London: Ian
Allan Publishing, 1985.

_____. *The Spitfire Story*. London: Arms &
Armour Press, 1982
Ramsey, Winston G. *The Battle of Britain—Then
& Now*. London: After the Battle
Publications, 1989.

Rawlings, John D. R. *The History of the Royal Air
Force*. Feltham, UK: Temple Press,
1984.

Taylor, John W. R. *Combat Aircraft of the World*.
New York: G. P. Putnam's Sons, 1969.

Thetford, Owen. *Aircraft of the Royal Air Force*.
London: Putnam, 1988.

Wood, Derek and Derek Dempster. *The Narrow
Margin*. London: Tri-Service Press,
1990.

Dan Patterson is a self-employed photographer, graphic designer, and private pilot living in Dayton, Ohio. Previous books are *Shoo Shoo Baby, A Lucky Lady of the Sky, The Lady: Boeing B-17 Flying Fortress, The Soldier: Consolidated B-24 Liberator, Mustang: North American P-51, Lancaster: RAF Heavy Bomber, Messerschmitt Bf 109: Luftwaffe Fighter,* and *American Eagles: A History of the United States Air Force.*

Ron Dick served for 38 years in the Royal Air Force, accumulating over 5,000 hours in more than 60 types of aircraft. He retired from the service as an Air Vice-Marshal in 1988 following a tour as the British Defence Attache in Washington, D.C. He now lives in Virginia, writing and lecturing generally on military and aviation history. Previous books are *Lancaster: RAF Heavy Bomber, Messerschmitt Bf 109: Luftwaffe Fighter,* and *American Eagles: A History of the United States Air Force.*